John Lennon
Voice of a Generation

Liz Gogerly

HODDER
Wayland

an imprint of Hodder Children's Books

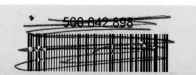

© 2002 White-Thomson Publishing Ltd

Produced for Hodder Wayland
by White-Thomson Publishing Ltd
2/3 St Andrew's Place, Lewes, BN7 1UP

Editor: Anna Lee
Inside and Cover Design: Tim Mayer
Picture Research: Shelley Noronha – Glass Onion Pictures
Proofreader: Lindsay Barnes

Cover: John Lennon on stage in New York in 1972.
Title page: John Lennon (from the cover of the 'Help!'
album, released in August 1965).

Published in Great Britain in 2002 by Hodder Wayland,
an imprint of Hodder Children's Books
This paperback edition published in 2004

The publisher would like to thank Yoko Ono for her kind
permission to use the following pictures:
8, 9, 13, 39, 40 © Yoko Ono.
Used by Permission/All Rights Reserved

Titles in this series:
Muhammad Ali: The Greatest
Neil Armstrong: The First Man on the Moon
Fidel Castro: Leader of Cuba's Revolution
Bill Gates: Computer Legend
Diana: The People's Princess
Martin Luther King Jr.: Civil Rights Hero
Nelson Mandela: Father of Freedom
Mother Teresa: Saint of the Slums
Pope John Paul II: Pope for the People
Pablo Picasso: Master of Modern Art
Queen Elizabeth II: Monarch of Our Times
The Queen Mother: Grandmother of a Nation
John Lennon: Voice of a Generation
Gandhi: The Peaceful Revolutionary
Florence Nightingale: The Lady of the Lamp
The Dalai Lama: Peacemaker from Tibet
Wolfgang Amadeus Mozart: Musical Genius
William Shakespeare: Poet and Playwright
Roald Dahl: The Storyteller
Elvis Presley: The King of Rock 'n' Roll
Vincent van Gogh: The Troubled Artist

British Library Cataloguing in Publication Data
Gogerly, Liz
   John Lennon. – (Famous lives)
   1.Lennon, John, 1940-1980 2.Singers – Great Britain –
   Biography – Juvenile literature 3.Rock musicians – Great
   Britain – Biography – Juvenile literature 4.Lyricists –
   Great Britain – Biography – Juvenile literature
   I.Title
   782.4'2'166'092

ISBN 0 7502 3948 4

Printed in Hong Kong

Hodder Children's Books
A division of Hodder Headline Limited
338 Euston Road, London, NW1 3BH

Picture acknowledgements
The publisher would like to thank the following for their
kind permission to use these pictures:
Associated Press 24, 25, 41; Camera Press 12, 33 (top);
Frank Gamma 38; Hulton Archive 13, 16, 17, 42,
45 (right); Pictorial Press Limited (title page), 6, 11, 21, 22,
27, 32, 43 (right), 44; Popperfoto 5, 23, 26, 28, 30, 35, 43
(left), 45 (left); Astrid Kirchherr/Redferns 14, 15, 18, 33
(bottom); Rex Features London 4, 19, 20, 29; Frank
Spooner Pictures 7, 38; Starfile (cover), 36, 37; Topham
Picturepoint 10, 34.

Contents

'Imagine'

It is May 1971, and John Lennon sits at a white baby grand piano in an all-white room. He starts to sing and a camera begins to roll. His wife Yoko Ono, dressed in white, drifts from window to window, opening the shutters and letting the light flood in. John gazes at the camera and sings the song for which he is most remembered. The simple words are a plea for world peace. The song is 'Imagine'. It is to become one of the most popular songs of the twentieth century.

'We hoped the act of songwriting could help better the world. That's what we believed. We felt our songs were honest, [that] whatever came out of us would definitely help because truth has its own power.'
Yoko Ono in the *Observer* newspaper, December 2000.

John never stopped loving rock 'n' roll. He arrived at a party in 1967 wearing a 1950s-style leather jacket.

John Lennon had come a long way from the angry young teenager in a black leather jacket. He was no longer the loveable rogue who had led the most successful band in pop history, the Beatles, either. Now he was just John and, together with Yoko, he hoped to spread a message of love and peace. This mission was cut short when he was murdered in New York in 1980. But the message lives on in his music and he remains one of rock's most inspirational and lasting heroes.

John relaxes with his wife Yoko Ono at their home near Ascot in England, in about 1970.

Growing up in Liverpool

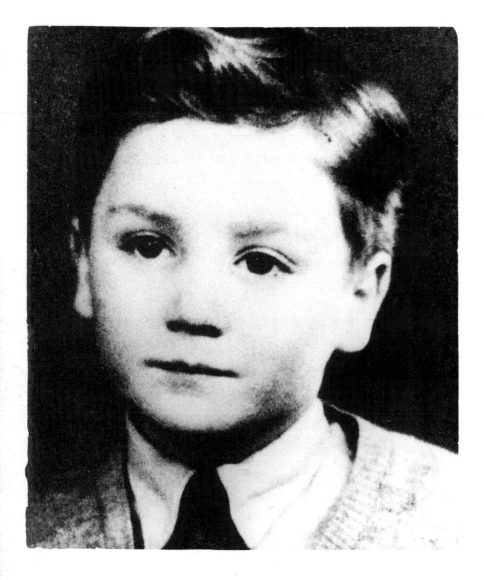

Even as a little boy, John knew he was different from other children. He spent hours reading and drawing by himself.

John was born on 9 October 1940 in Liverpool, England. He was the only child of Alfred and Julia Lennon. Alfred was a sailor, so he was often away from home, but Julia filled their home with music and jokes. At the time, Britain was in the middle of the Second World War (1939-45) and the industrial town of Liverpool was heavily bombed. The once great port could no longer provide jobs for its large number of workers, so there was high unemployment. Yet although these were tough times, there was still a great sense of pride in the city.

The Lennons lived in a working-class area called Penny Lane, which was immortalized in the Beatles' song, 'Penny Lane'. Throughout his life John never forgot that he was from Liverpool. In many ways it was a rough town, but growing up there gave John an honesty and sense of humour that came through in his music.

When John was four, his parents separated. John wanted to live with his mother, but eventually she decided that her sister Mimi and husband George could give him a more stable background.

Aunt Mimi and Uncle George lived in a middle-class area of Liverpool called Woolton. John loved his Uncle and Auntie, and they tried to keep his childhood as normal as it could be with a father away at sea and a mother who eventually set up home with another man.

'My childhood was not all suffering. It was not all slum. I was always well dressed, well fed, well schooled, and brought up to be a nice lower-middle-class English boy.'
John Lennon from *Last Interview: All We Are Saying – John Lennon and Yoko Ono* by David Sheff.

John aged eight with his mother Julia on one of her visits. They shared a love of music and a great sense of humour.

The Young Rebel

George and Mimi doted on their young nephew. George was like a father to John and each night he'd sit him on his knee and read him the newspaper. John started to read and write when he was four, and his love of newspapers lasted throughout his life. His mother, Julia, would visit occasionally but John still felt abandoned. This pain was echoed years later in his song 'Mother'.

John with his Aunt Mimi. She adored her nephew and treated him as her son.

John outside his childhood home in Liverpool, aged about ten.

When he was five John went to Dovedale Primary, where he soon stood out as the bad boy. John didn't join in the games in the playground. He liked to create his own fun and become the centre of attention. If he wasn't in fights, he was thinking of ways to shock the other children. He particularly liked playing jokes and teasing people with his cruel humour.

John did well in most subjects at school except maths. He was especially good at art. He also loved music, and, when he was eight, he started to play the harmonica. At age eleven, John passed the exam that won him a place at one of Liverpool's top schools, Quarry Bank Grammar School. As a reward, George bought him a brand new bicycle.

Rock 'n' Roll!

From the moment John arrived at Quarry Bank Grammar School he rebelled. He'd skip lessons and talk back to the teachers. He liked to be scruffy and usually wore his school uniform all creased up. With the hard rules and strict teachers at Quarry Bank, John was asking for trouble. Although he often had bad reports and detentions, John still shone in art, and enjoyed reading and writing stories and poems.

Throughout his teenage years John wrote stories and poems and drew cartoons. The influence of rock 'n' roll is obvious in these drawings he did when he was sixteen.

When John was fifteen, he first heard rock 'n' roll. With rhythmic guitars, double bass and drums, this new kind of music from the United States was unlike anything John had heard before. The American performer, Elvis Presley, was the king of rock 'n' roll and John wanted to be just like him. Within months he transformed himself – he greased back his hair and wore tight trousers and thick-soled shoes.

All John needed now was a guitar. He eventually bought himself one by mail order and formed a band at school – they called themselves the Quarry Men. School wasn't important any more, and when John failed all his exams in 1957, he didn't care – rock 'n' roll was all that mattered!

The King of rock 'n' roll, Elvis Presley. John later said: 'Without Elvis there would be no Beatles.'

Meeting Paul McCartney

In July 1957 the Quarry Men played a garden fair at St Peter's Parish Church in Liverpool. In the crowd, a fifteen-year-old boy with dark hair watched with interest. He also played the guitar and was struck by John's wild performance. His name was Paul McCartney. He shared John's passion for rock 'n' roll, and when he picked up a guitar to show the Quarry Men what he could do, they were impressed. A few days later, John asked him to join the band.

'That was the day, the day that I met Paul, that it started moving.' John Lennon in *The Beatles Anthology* by the Beatles.

John leading the Quarry Men at a church fair.

George, John and Paul outside Paul's house in about 1960. They'd skip school and college to practise while Paul's dad was at work.

Later that summer, John started at Liverpool College of Art. Here he explored all kinds of art, including graphic design and painting. He had more freedom than at school, and work was still the last thing on John's mind. Music, closely followed by girls, was his main interest, and he was also becoming good friends with Paul. Paul liked to study and he played the guitar better than John, but the differences between them didn't seem to matter. Soon, they began writing songs together.

Paul's friend George Harrison, joined the band in early 1958. Things were going well, until John's mother, Julia, was knocked down and killed by a car. For John, this tragedy was a terrible blow. In recent years he'd become closer to his mother – she even liked rock 'n' roll music. With her death, he felt as if he'd lost her for the second time in his life. Paul understood John's grief because his mother had died too, and the bond between the two young men grew stronger.

The Beatles are Born

When John met Cynthia she looked quite conservative. She soon dyed her hair blond so she would look like John's favourite French actress, Brigitte Bardot.

John met his future wife, Cynthia Powell, at a college Christmas dance in 1958. This quiet, polite girl, who didn't smoke or drink, didn't seem John's type. Nor did his handsome best friend, Stuart Sutcliffe, who was sensitive and one of the most promising artists at college. Both relationships revealed the softer side of John.

In June 1960 Stuart bought a bass guitar and joined the Quarry Men. With drummer Pete Best on board, the line-up was complete. They renamed the band the Beatals, then changed it to the Silver Beetles, before finally settling on the Beatles. At first they played youth clubs and dance halls in Liverpool. Then, in autumn 1960, the Beatles had their first break when they were invited to play the Kaiserkeller club in Hamburg. The combination of John's raw vocals and Paul's smoother style took the audience by storm. The band played for eight hours each night, before returning to a cramped little room to grab a few hours' sleep.

A moody picture of George, Stuart and John taken in Hamburg. Most bands at this time were smartly dressed but the Beatles often didn't shave and wore creased clothes.

When the Beatles arrived back in Liverpool in December, they'd become confident professionals and were ready to change the history of rock 'n' roll music.

> '*Our best work was never recorded ... what we generated* [live on stage in Hamburg and Liverpool] *was fantastic when we played straight rock* [early rock 'n' roll based on beat and rhythmic guitar] *and there was nobody to touch us in Britain.*'
>
> John Lennon, in *Lennon Remembers* by Jann S. Wenner.

The Cavern

On their return from Hamburg, the Beatles started to play regularly in a small club in Liverpool called the Cavern. Over the next two and half years they would play there 292 times. Their set was made up of covers from other rock 'n' roll bands. In their creased black polo necks and black leather jackets, they were especially popular with the girls. Some were drawn to Paul's good looks, while others were attracted to John, who poured his heart and soul into the music.

Brian Epstein owned a record shop in Liverpool. By late 1961, a steady stream of customers had asked for a record by the Beatles, and Brian decided to find out more about this popular band. When he saw them play, he immediately recognized their talent.

John playing at the Cavern Club in Liverpool. It is a dark, damp cellar with a tiny stage, but the Beatles played some of their best live music there.

They looked a mess, they ate and smoked on stage and swore at the audience, but their music and their humour was impressive. He believed he could find them a record deal if they would agree to let him manage them.

The Beatles were surprised that this wealthy man was interested in them, but decided to trust him. As manager, Brian tackled their image first. New suits and haircuts gave them a more polished look. He also encouraged them to write and perform their own songs.

Brian Epstein, who helped the Beatles achieve their incredible success.

'Brian put us in neat suits and shirts and Paul was right behind him. I didn't dig that and I tried to get George to rebel with me. I'd say to George, "Look, we don't need these suits. Let's chuck them out of the window." ' John Lennon in *Lennon – The Definitive Biography*.

1962: The Year it All Happened

1962 was a year of highs and lows for John. In April Stuart Sutcliffe died suddenly from a brain haemorrhage. John was deeply affected by the death of his best friend and poured himself into his work. The Beatles continued to play live and returned to Hamburg. While they were there, Brian sent a telegram with the wonderful news that the record label EMI wanted to give them a contract. They returned home to record their first single, 'Love Me Do'. It was a simple, catchy song, written by John and Paul when they were teenagers, and it became their first hit in October of that year.

John (right) and Paul would become the most famous songwriting partnership of all time. John said there was nothing original about what they were doing, it was just rock 'n' roll music.

In August, John had another shock – Cynthia was pregnant. In the 1960s if a girl was pregnant her boyfriend was expected to 'do the right thing' and marry her. Their wedding was quick and without fuss at a registry office. John had to leave early to play at a concert in Chester.

> '*I thought it would be goodbye to the group, getting married. But I did feel embarrassed, walking about, married. It was like walking about with odd socks on or your fly open.*' John Lennon in *The Beatles Anthology*.

Throughout their marriage, John had to juggle being a husband and father with being a Beatle. This was especially difficult because Brian Epstein had decided that fans preferred to believe that all the Beatles were single. As a result, John and Cynthia had to keep their marriage secret from the public. At the time it was quite common for married popstars to claim they were single, but keeping up the pretence could be very stressful. For John, it meant that being a Beatle usually came before being a husband and father.

John shares a rare moment with his son Julian. He was on tour when Julian was born in April 1963 and would hardly see his son in the years to come.

Beatlemania

When the Beatles made their first album, 'Please Please Me', Ringo Starr was brought in to replace the drummer Pete Best. John liked Pete, but Brian felt he didn't fit in with the other personalities in the band. The single 'Please Please Me' went to number one in the UK in March 1963 and more tours of the UK followed. 'She Loves You' also went to the top of the British charts in September and the Beatles drew enormous crowds of screaming fans wherever they went.

The Beatles were the first major 'boy band'. At concerts the fans would cry out and cheer for their favourite Beatle. John stood out as the most intellectual member of the band.

The Beatles playing the UK television show 'Top of the Pops' in 1964. John is on the far left. In the same year they made their debut on US television.

Television appearances stirred up the new sensation that was labelled 'Beatlemania'. By February 1964, Beatlemania had spread to the USA. When 'I Want To Hold Your Hand' reached number one in the USA, the Beatles made their first trip across the Atlantic.

'It's like we're four freaks being wheeled out to be seen, shake our heads about, and get back in our cage afterwards.'
John Lennon in *Lennon – the Definitive Biography*.

John had dreamed of becoming a bigger star than Elvis, but sudden fame had its drawbacks. Rather than seeing the world, the Beatles saw the inside of hotels, tour buses and limousines. During this period they spent little time at home and for John this meant being away from his new son, Julian, for months at a time. John became more and more unhappy. Being a Beatle was no longer about the music.

The Outspoken Beatle

The album 'Help!' was released in August 1965 at the same time as the Beatle's second film, 'Help!'.

In the early days of the Beatles, John and Paul enjoyed writing together and signed a deal that meant all songs would be credited to Lennon/McCartney. Gradually, they started to write their own songs and two distinct styles emerged. Paul liked more romantic songs such as the ballad 'Yesterday'. John's lyrics were often about personal experiences and were crafted more like poetry. In 'Strawberry Fields Forever' and 'In My Life', John looked back on his days growing up in Liverpool. The catchy pop song, 'Help' voiced John's growing insecurity about being a Beatle.

John was always the most outspoken Beatle. The humour that had seen him through school would come out in interviews or during performances. It was a great surprise when, in June 1965, each of the Beatles was awarded an MBE (Member of the Order of the British Empire) by the Queen. MBEs are medals that are usually given to people for doing charity work or being a war hero. The Beatles received theirs because of their international success.

John wasn't impressed and many people were angry with the way he spoke out to the press (see box). From then on, John became more political and ready to voice his opinions.

The Beatles collected their MBEs from Buckingham Palace in October 1965. John gave his MBE to his Aunt Mimi.

'Lots of people who complained about us receiving the MBE received theirs for heroism in the war – for killing people. We received ours for entertaining other people. I'd say we deserve ours more.'
John Lennon on receiving an MBE.

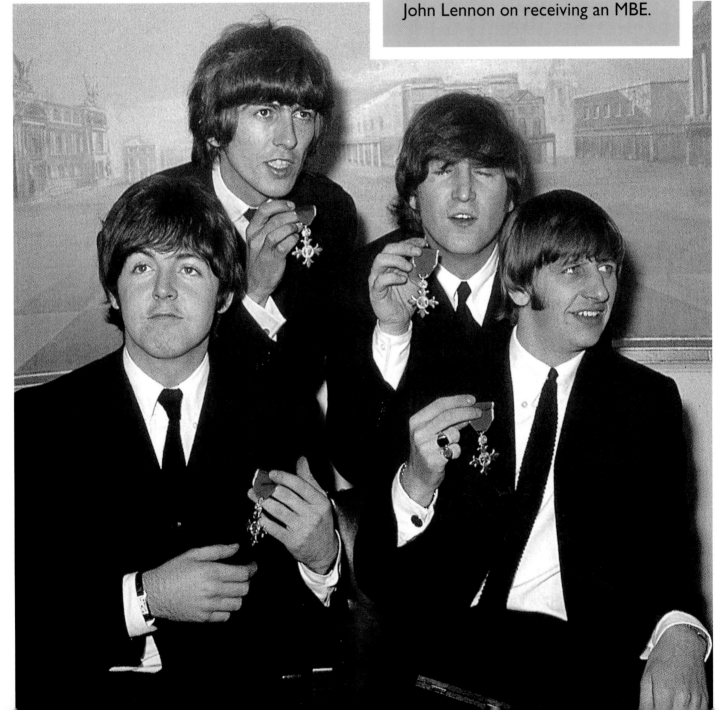

'Bigger Than Jesus'

In 1966 John found himself in trouble again. In an interview with a London newspaper he revealed his views on society (see box). When the interview was released in the USA, his meaning was misunderstood. The American media claimed that John was saying that the Beatles were more important than Jesus Christ.

John apologizes for his comment about the Beatles being bigger than Jesus during a press conference in Chicago.

> **'Christianity will go. It will vanish and shrink. I needn't argue about that. I'm right and I will be proved right. We're more popular than Jesus now; I don't know which will go first – rock 'n' roll or Christianity.'**
> John Lennon in the *Evening Standard* newspaper, 4 March 1966.

The Beatles play one of their last live gigs at New York's Shea Stadium on 23 August 1966. The crowd was ecstatic but the Beatles no longer enjoyed playing live.

The backlash was enormous. People who didn't like modern music saw this as proof that bands such as the Beatles were a bad influence on teenagers. Some fans turned against the Beatles and burned all their records. To make matters worse, death threats were made against them. With an American tour about to begin, the situation was desperate.

John was upset by the whole business. At a press conference in Chicago he tried to explain what he had meant. The tour went ahead, but the Beatles were scared. On 29 August 1966 the Beatles played their last concert ever in Candlestick Park in San Francisco, USA. They'd once loved the stage but now the screams of the fans were so loud that they couldn't hear themselves sing or play. It seemed the right time to quit live performances. They would play live together one more time but the circumstances would be very different.

'All You Need is Love'

Yoko Ono photographed at one of her art shows in October 1967. This exhibit is called 'Half a Bedroom'. John was inspired by her simple and direct style.

Playing live had always been John's biggest thrill. With that gone, he looked for something new and exciting to fill the gap. In late 1966 he visited an art exhibition in London. It was here that he met Yoko Ono for the first time. Although he was still married to Cynthia, John became very interested in the tiny Japanese artist with the mop of thick black hair. He liked her art and particularly enjoyed her exhibit with a ladder leading up to the ceiling. He climbed the ladder and, using a spyglass, read Yoko's tiny message. It said, 'YES'. John had found someone who thought like him.

The cover for the Sgt. Peppers album was a collage of the Beatle's own heroes. John chose the authors Oscar Wilde, Lewis Carroll and Edgar Allan Poe.

By 1967 the Beatles had changed their image once again. They dressed in brightly coloured clothes and grew their hair. They became interested in Indian religions and experimented with different types of music and with drugs. When they released the 'Sgt Peppers' album, nobody had heard anything quite like it before. It topped the charts and is regarded (by some) as John and Paul's creative peak. Later that year, the Beatles released the single 'All You Need is Love'. In the USA, young people were protesting against the war in Vietnam. 'All You Need is Love' expressed the mood of the time perfectly.

'We [the Beatles] were part of whatever the Sixties was. It was happening itself. We were the ones chosen to represent what was going on on the street'.
John Lennon in *The Beatles Anthology*.

The Beginning of the End

When Brian Epstein died suddenly in August 1967, the Beatles were stunned. Without their manager, the differences between the band members, especially John and Paul, started to matter. John believed that Paul tried to take over the band at this point. Disastrous business ventures, such as setting up their own company, Apple Corps, deepened the divisions. The idea behind Apple was that the Beatles would fund individuals such as artists or musicians, but it was to cost them a lot of money.

'After Brian died, we collapsed. Paul took over and supposedly led us, you know. But what is leading us when we went round in circles?' John Lennon, from *Lennon Remembers.*

The Apple Boutique in the centre of London was opened in December 1967. It sold clothes, books and records and was just one part of Apple Corps.

The Beatles with the Maharishi. John said meditation brought relaxation and understanding.

Throughout this time John was becoming closer to Yoko Ono. John and the other Beatles became more interested in meditation and eastern religions, too. In early 1968 they visited the guru, Maharishi, in India. This break made John question his own beliefs, his life as a Beatle and also his marriage. By the time the Beatles returned to England, John had decided to leave Cynthia. John and Yoko now went everywhere together – including the Beatles' recording sessions. The other Beatles weren't happy. They didn't like the influence that Yoko seemed to have on John. Soon, the break-up of the Beatles became inevitable.

'Give Peace a Chance'

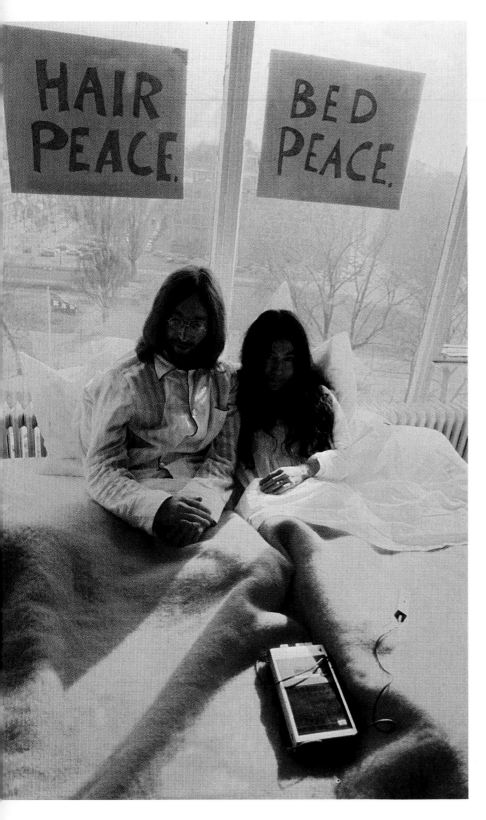

John wanted more out of life than being a Beatle. Yoko helped him see the world through different eyes, and he believed that together they could spread a message of peace. In March 1969 they took a plane to Gibraltar and were married. From then on they swore to do everything together – as artists, and as husband and wife. John changed his name to John Ono Lennon. Many people who knew him felt that he'd become a different person.

Five days after their marriage John and Yoko staged 'Bed Peace'. They booked into the presidential suite at the Amsterdam Hilton hotel and for one week they sat up in bed and gave interviews to promote world peace. John's hair had grown and he asked others to grow their hair as a sign of support. The media loved it and it became the most talked about honeymoon ever.

John and Yoko at the Amsterdam Hilton hotel during 'Bed Peace'.

'Really, there's no difference between what we're doing now and what we've always done. The idea of peace has always been with us. You could smell it in the early Beatle songs. It's like the Beatles singing 'All You Need is Love' – I'm just singing 'All You Need is Peace' now.' John Lennon talking about 'Bed Peace', in *The Beatles Anthology*.

John and Yoko's peace poster stands out in a New York street. In December 1971, their song 'Happy Xmas (War is Over)' repeated the message.

Later, John and Yoko recorded 'Give Peace a Chance'. At Christmas, they placed posters on billboards in eleven cities across the word with the slogan: 'WAR IS OVER! If you want it. Happy Christmas from John and Yoko'. John also returned his MBE to the Queen in protest against the war in Vietnam.

The Dream is Over

In January 1969 the Beatles recorded the album 'Let it Be'. While they played, a film was recorded. John said it was 'six weeks of misery' and the film shows the frustration and distance between John and Paul. That summer, the Beatles recorded their final album together. Despite the arguments, 'Abbey Road' contained some of the best songs ever recorded by the Beatles. John's song 'Come Together' was a freedom song and became the Beatles' last great anthem.

All the Beatles grew their hair for the cover of their album 'Let It Be'. Unlike their previous albums, the Beatles weren't photographed as a group.

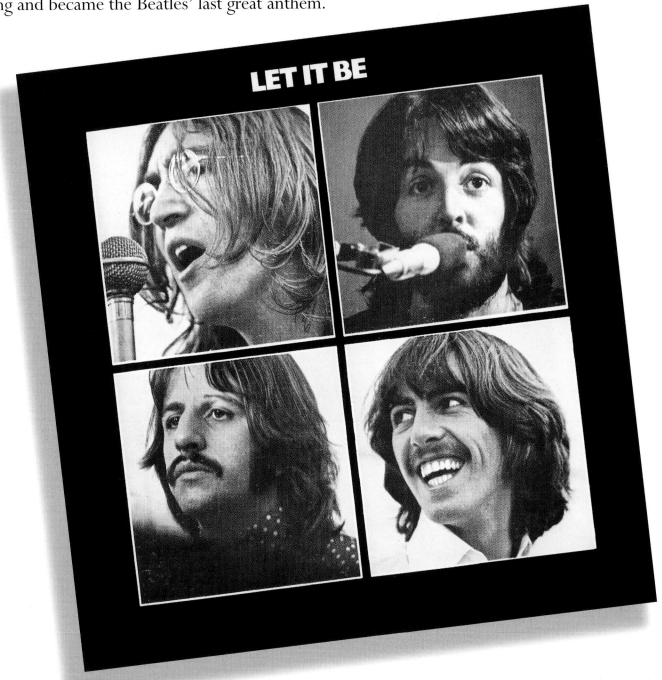

32

One grey day in January 1969 the Beatles played their first live performance in over two years. It was also to be their last. This extraordinary event was staged on the roof of the Apple studios in central London. When they began playing, the crowds of people below couldn't believe their ears – nobody had done anything like this before. After five songs, the police made them stop – it was somehow a fitting end. Although John had talked about leaving the band, it was Paul who announced the split in April 1970. Yoko was blamed by the other band members, which made John angry – he and Paul wouldn't speak for years.

The Beatles playing live on the roof of the Apple studios on 30 January 1969. They played on even when they heard the police would arrest them.

During the early years of their marriage John and Yoko were always together. 'The only thing that could split us is death,' John said.

'It's just natural. It's not a great disaster. People keep talking about it as if it's the end of the earth. It's only a rock group that split up. It's nothing important. You have all the old records there if you want to reminisce. You have all this great music.' John Lennon talking about the end of the Beatles in *The Beatles Anthology*.

33

Plastic Ono Band

Fans mourned the loss of the Beatles, but for John it was a new beginning. He retired to a beautiful white Georgian manor house near Ascot in England. With its large gardens, John and Yoko found peace and quiet for a while. John was still behind the peace movement and also became interested in communism. Although he had become more gentle and sensitive, to many people he represented everything that was anti-establishment – and they either loved him or hated him for this.

Fans had the same love-hate relationship with John and Yoko's music. Some people liked the new direction John was taking, while others missed the Beatles. In late 1970 John and Yoko released the 'John Lennon/Plastic Ono Band' album. For John this was an opportunity to reflect upon his life. In 'Mother' he remembered the mother he claimed he lost twice, once when he was a child and again when she died. In 'Working Class Hero' he rejected the British class system. The following year they released the album, 'Imagine'.

John and Yoko in the library at their home in Tittenhurst. John was a great reader and liked to collect old leatherbound books.

In the title track he asked his listeners to imagine a peaceful world with no religion or material possessions. Some people asked how a millionaire could talk about having nothing.

'If you can imagine a world at peace, with no denominations of religion – not without religion but without this my-God-is-bigger-than-your-God thing – then it can be true.'
John Lennon talking about his song 'Imagine' in *Last Interview: All We Are Saying – John Lennon and Yoko Ono.*

John and Yoko supported other political movements. In 1970 they cut their hair for a charity auction held by the 'Black Power' movement.

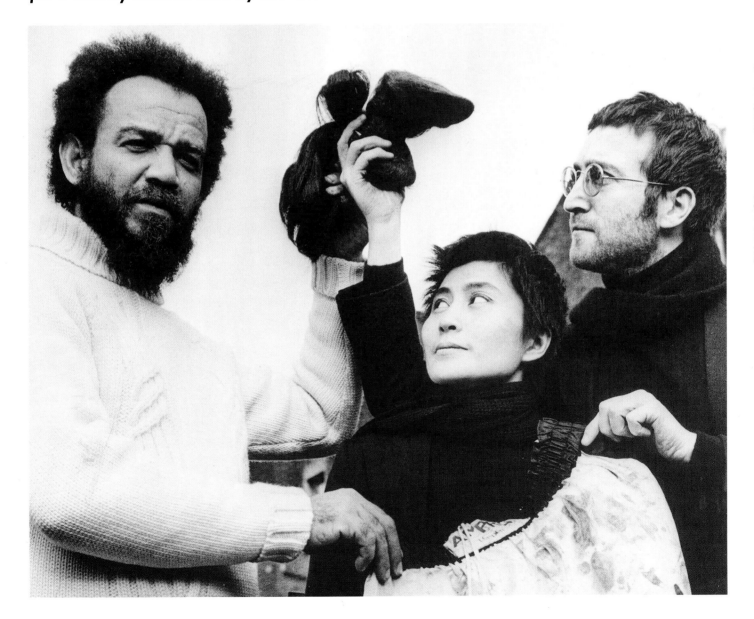

New York and Los Angeles

In 1971 John and Yoko moved to New York – John would never return to Britain again. In New York he could walk the streets without fans bothering him. It was an exciting city, and John was inspired to make music again. In December 'Happy Xmas, War is Over' was released. But there was something missing – John wanted to play live again.

John needed a work permit to play live in the United States. With his political leanings and open-minded approach to drugs, the United States authorities were cautious about giving him the permit. John found a way around the problem by playing charity events. However, when he played benefit gigs for political prisoners, the Federal Bureau of Investigation (FBI) opened a file on his movements. There was a genuine fear that John had the power to stir up anti-establishment feelings. As a result, the threat of deportation hung over his head for the next few years.

John at the Statue of Liberty in New York. 'America is where it's at,' he told a Rolling Stone journalist.

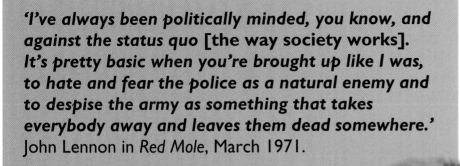

'*I've always been politically minded, you know, and against the status quo* [the way society works]. *It's pretty basic when you're brought up like I was, to hate and fear the police as a natural enemy and to despise the army as something that takes everybody away and leaves them dead somewhere.*'
John Lennon in *Red Mole*, March 1971.

John on stage in New York in 1972. It was fantastic to be playing live again.

This wasn't his only problem – by 1973 his marriage to Yoko was in trouble. John left their New York apartment and moved to Los Angeles. For the next two years, he tried to find comfort in drugs and alcohol.

'Beautiful Boy'

John and Yoko had always wanted a child together. When they were re-united in early 1975, Yoko soon became pregnant. John decided to retire from music temporarily to concentrate upon being a father. He also started to write a book called *Sky Writing By Word of Mouth*.

In October 1975, after years of legal battles, the order for John's deportation was dropped. The next day, on John's own birthday, Sean Taro Ono Lennon was born. On returning from the hospital Yoko handed Sean to John and told him, 'I've carried him for the last few months. Now it's your turn.'

John and Yoko lived on the seventh floor of the Gothic-looking Dakota building in New York.

Yoko nearly died during childbirth. John believed Sean's safe delivery was a miracle and the child was a gift to him and Yoko.

John enjoyed his new role as a father. He'd missed his first son Julian growing up and poured his love into Sean. Sean slept between his parents and John fed, washed and looked after him in every way. John even started to study cookery books! For five years he was happy to play Dad while Yoko took care of the business side of life. Yoko proved to be better at business than John. As well as investing in property, one of Yoko's many ventures was a farm that supplied the Lennon's strict organic dietary needs. In July 1976 John was finally given legal permission to live and work in the United States.

'Starting Over'

John loved music too much to be away from it for long. In 1980 he released a new album called 'Double Fantasy'. Gone was the angry young man; John seemed content and happy with his life. In the first single, 'Starting Over', he expressed his joy at returning to recording. The song 'Beautiful Boy' was about Sean and revealed his deep feelings about being a father. At last, John had found the inner peace he'd always craved, and could leave behind the bigger issues such as world peace.

'The hardest thing is facing yourself. It's easier to shout 'Revolution' and 'Power to the People' than it is to look at yourself and try to find out what's real inside you and what isn't, when you're pulling the wool over your own eyes.'
John Lennon in *Rolling Stone* magazine, 1980.

John with his son Sean at their home in New York. John loved taking care of Sean.

John was forty now, and was excited about his future. He was building a relationship with Julian, a bond that grew stronger because Julian was showing a talent for music. He was also friends with the other Beatles. Although he never saw Auntie Mimi, they often had long telephone calls. John missed the British sense of humour and Mimi sent him videos of the classic British comedies 'Fawlty Towers' and 'Monty Python'. He told her he was feeling homesick and was planning to visit England. He talked about a mini comeback tour of Britain, the US and Hamburg. John wanted to see the places that had shaped his life once more.

John and Yoko outside the studio where they recorded 'Double Fantasy'. They look relaxed and happy about their comeback.

Shot Five Times

John had always felt safe in New York. The autograph-hunters were polite and fans didn't bother him. On Monday 8 December 1980 there didn't seem any reason to feel differently. John and Yoko had more interviews with the media than usual, but that was to be expected with the release of 'Double Fantasy'. They had no idea that a young man called Mark Chapman had been tracing their movements for a week.

> '*Mahatma Gandhi and Martin Luther King are great examples of fantastic non-violents who died violently. I can never work that out. We're pacifists, but I'm not sure what it means when you're such a pacifist that you get shot. I can never understand that.*'
> John Lennon in *Last Interview: All We Are Saying – John Lennon and Yoko Ono.*

John signing an autograph in September 1980. In December John signed Mark Chapman's copy of 'Double Fantasy'.

Mark Chapman as a teenager. In those days he was a fan of John Lennon and the Beatles.

JOHN LENNON SHOT DEAD

Gunned down by 'screwball' outside home as wife Yoko watches in horror

At about 4pm John signed an autograph for Chapman outside their apartment. John looked up when he'd finished signing and asked, 'Is that all? Do you want anything else?' Chapman later said he felt that John had known he was looking his killer in the eyes. John and Yoko then went to the studio. They arrived home at about 10.52pm. As they approached their apartment block, John saw Chapman hiding in the shadows. As he walked past him, Chapman withdrew a gun and shot John five times in the back. Amazingly, John was still alive. He was rushed to hospital in the back of a police car. However, his time had run out, and John was pronounced dead at 11.07pm.

John Lennon's death made newspaper headlines across the world. Everywhere people were united in grief.

The Message Lives On

As the news of John's death spread across the world, people struggled to understand Chapman's motives. They also tried to come to terms with the loss of John. Most people who remember that tragic day recall where they were and how they felt. On 14 December 1980, crowds gathered in cities around the world for a day of mourning. At 7pm in the UK and 2pm in New York people observed 10 minutes of silence. Throughout the day, radio stations everywhere played John's music.

On 14 December 1980, in John's hometown of Liverpool, 25,000 mourners flooded St George's Hall Plateau.

In New York fans gathered to mourn their hero. Yoko released the following statement: 'Bless you for your tears and prayers. I saw John smiling in the sky. I saw sorrow changing into clarity.'

The memory still burns bright. In Prague, the capital of the Czech Republic, fans light candles to mark the anniversary of the death of the legendary Beatle.

'I think that in many ways he was a simple Liverpool man right to the end. In our fourteen years together he never stopped trying to improve himself from within. We were best friends but also competitive artists. To me, he is still alive. Death alone doesn't extinguish a flame and a spirit like John.'
Yoko Ono speaking of John's death, from *Lennon – The Definitive Biography.*

By the end of the year, the single 'Starting Over' and album 'Double Fantasy' were number one in the UK and the US. 'Imagine' later topped the charts, and has reappeared in the British charts in 1988 and 1999. In 1995/96 the remaining Beatles released three albums of previously unreleased Beatles material. 'Real Love' and 'Free as a Bird' were of particular interest, as they were recorded by John in the 1970s. Paul, George and Ringo had re-mixed them and added their instruments and vocals. For the first time in over two decades the Beatles had been reunited.

In many ways, John will always be here, in his music, and his words. John would have been happy with that – he'd often said the message was all that mattered.

Glossary

Anti-establishment To be against people who make rules, or laws, such as the government.

Arrogant To think you are better than others and believe you are always right.

Autograph A famous person's hand-written signature.

Backlash The response to an event.

Billboards A large board for advertisements.

Brain haemorrhage Severe bleeding of the brain.

Communism A belief that the houses, land, factories and companies in a country should be run to profit everyone.

Cramped Describes a place where there isn't enough room for everyone and everything.

Debut The first public appearance or release.

Deport To send somebody back to their own country.

Detention When a child is forced to stay after school as a punishment.

Ecstatic Feeling of great happiness.

Exhibit A work of art that is on show at an exhibition.

Graphic design The layout of pictures, photos and words, produced by a designer for commercial purposes – as seen in books, magazines and posters or on packaging such as record covers.

Guru A religious teacher in the Hindu faith, or an influential person.

Harmonica A small musical instrument that is played by blowing air into a mouthpiece.

Immortalized To live for ever – or to be famous for ever.

Inevitable Something that is sure to happen.

Inspiration Something or someone that influences other people.

Line-up The people who make up a band.

Meditation Relaxation through deep breathing and mind control.

Motive The reason for doing something.

Outspoken To be open about feelings or beliefs – to give an opinion frankly and freely.

Press conference An interview with journalists.

Rebel To fight against government or people in charge.

Rhythmic A sound that has a regular beat.

Rogue A mischievous person who breaks rules.

Set The songs played by a band at a concert.

Shutters A wooden cover for a window.

Telegram A written message that can be sent quickly by radio. Often used to send urgent news or congratulations on special occasions.

Transform To make a great change in something.

Further Information

Books to read
Younger readers:
John Lennon by Harriet Castor (Franklin Watts, 2002)
Profiles: John Lennon by Paul Dowswell (Heinemann, 2001)
Real Love: the Drawings for Sean by John Lennon (illustrator) and Yoko Ono (Little, Brown and Company, 1999)
The Life and World of: John Lennon by Brian Williams (Heinemann Library, 2003)

By John Lennon:
In His Own Write/A Spaniard in the Works (Pimlico, 1997)
Sky Writing by Word of Mouth (Harper Collins, 1996)
Sources:
Last Interview: All We Are Saying – John Lennon and Yoko Ono by David Sheff (Sidgwick and Jackson, 2000)
Lennon – The Definitive Biography by Ray Coleman (Pan, 2000)
Lennon Remembers by Janns S. Wenner (Verso, 2000)
The Beatles Anthology by the Beatles (Cassel and Co., 2000)

Date Chart

1940, 9 October John Winston Lennon is born in Liverpool, England.

1945, September John goes to Dovedale Primary School, Liverpool.

1946 John moves in with Auntie Mimi and Uncle George.

1952, September John goes to Quarry Bank High School.

1955, 5 June John's Uncle George dies.

1957, May John starts his first band, the Quarry Men.

July John meets Paul McCartney, and invites him to join the band.

September Johns starts at Liverpool College of Art.

1958, February George Harrison joins the Quarry Men.

15 July Julia Lennon is knocked over by a car and killed.

1960, May The Quarry Men tour for the first time.

June The Quarry Men become the Beatles.

July John leaves Liverpool College of Art.

August–December The Beatles play live in Hamburg.

1961, 21 March The Beatles play at the Cavern Club for the first time.

3 December Brian Epstein becomes manager of the Beatles.

1962, 10 April Stuart Sutcliffe dies.

9 May The Beatles sign with EMI.

18 August Ringo Starr joins the Beatles.

23 August John marries Cynthia Powell.

5 October 'Love Me Do' is released.

1963, 2 March 'Please Please Me' goes to number one in the UK.

8 April Julian Lennon is born.

1964, 1 February 'I Want To Hold Your Hand' goes to number one in the US.

7 February The Beatles start their first US tour.

1965, 26 October The Beatles receive MBEs at Buckingham Palace.

1966, 4 March John's famous 'The Beatles are bigger than Jesus Christ' interview appears in the *Evening Standard*.

31 July Radio stations in the US ban all Beatles music.

29 August The last Beatles concert at Candlestick Park in San Francisco.

9 November John meets Yoko Ono.

1967, 1 June 'Sgt. Pepper's Lonely Hearts Club Band' is released.

27 August Brian Epstein dies.

November Cynthia Lennon divorces John.

1969, January The Beatles play their last live performance in London.

20 March John marries Yoko Ono in Gibraltar.

25–31 March John and Yoko's 'Bed-in For Peace' in Amsterdam.

4 July John releases his first solo single, 'Give Peace A Chance'.

1970, 10 April Paul McCartney annouces he's leaving the Beatles.

1971, 3 September John and Yoko leave England to live in New York.

8 October 'Imagine' is released.

1973, October John and Yoko decide to split up. John moves to Los Angeles.

1975, January John is re-united with Yoko.

9 October Sean Taro Ono Lennon is born.

1976, 27 July John's application to become a resident of the USA is accepted.

1980, 17 November 'Double Fantasy' album is released.

8 December (9 December in the UK) John is shot dead by Mark Chapman.

10 December John is cremated in New York.

2001, 30th November George Harrison dies from cancer in Los Angeles in the United States.

Index

All page numbers in **bold** refer to pictures as well as text.